Contents

Making fun baby afghans is easy with the corner to corner crochet technique! The diagonal construction eliminates the need for a tedious long starting chain, and the basic block pattern lets you create colorful charted images.

LEISURE ARTS, INC. • Maumelle, Arkansas

Anchor

EASY

Finished Size: 33¼" x 44½" (84.5 cm x 113 cm)

SHOPPING LIST

Yarn (Medium Weight) MEDIUM 4

[5 ounces, 256 yards

(141 grams, 234 meters) per skein]:

- ☐ Off White - 5 skeins
- ☐ Navy - 2 skeins
- ☐ Red - 1 skein

Crochet Hook

- ☐ Size I (5.5 mm)

  or size needed for gauge

Additional Supplies

- ☐ Bobbins

GAUGE INFORMATION

4 Blocks (side by side) = 3" (7.5 cm)

Gauge Swatch: 3¼" x 3¼" x 4½"

(8.25 cm x 8.25 cm x 11.5 cm)

Work same as Body for 4 rows: 4 Blocks.

STITCH GUIDE

BEGINNING BLOCK

Ch 6, turn; dc in fourth ch from hook and in next 2 chs.

BLOCK

Slip st in ch-3 sp of previous Block ***(Fig. A)***, ch 3, 3 dc in same sp ***(Fig. B)***.

Fig. A

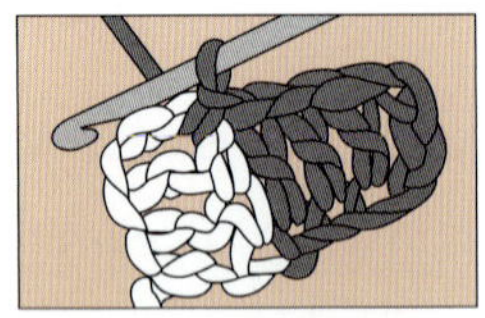

Fig. B

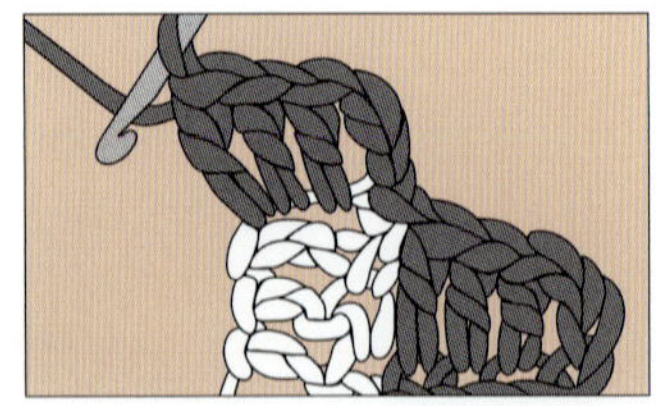

BODY

Body is worked diagonally.

Row 1 (Right side)**:** With Off White, ch 6, dc in fourth ch from hook and in last 2 chs: one Block.

Note: Loop a short piece of yarn around any stitch to mark Row 1 as **right** side **and** bottom corner.

Row 2: Work Beginning Block, slip st in ch-3 sp on first Block, ch 3, 3 dc in same sp: 2 Blocks.

Row 3: Work Beginning Block, slip st in ch-3 sp on first Block, ch 3, 3 dc in same sp, work Block: 3 Blocks.

Rows 4-24: Work Beginning Block, slip st in ch-3 sp on first Block, ch 3, 3 dc in same sp, work Blocks across: 24 Blocks.

Row 25: Work Beginning Block, slip st in ch-3 sp on first Block, ch 3, 3 dc in same sp, work 4 Blocks changing to Navy in last dc made ***(Fig. 1c, page 22)***, work 8 Blocks changing to Off White in last dc made, work Blocks across: 25 Blocks.

Always change colors in same manner, using bobbins for small sections of color. Keep unused color to **wrong** side of work; do **not** cut yarn until color is no longer needed.

Continue to follow Chart throughout.

Rows 26-43: Work Beginning Block, slip st in ch-3 sp on first Block, ch 3, 3 dc in same sp, work Blocks across: 43 Blocks.

Row 44: Turn; slip st in first 3 dc and in next ch-3 sp, ch 3, 3 dc in same sp, work Blocks across.

Row 45: Work Beginning Block, slip st in ch-3 sp on first Block, ch 3, 3 dc in same sp, work Blocks across to last Block, slip st in ch-3 sp on last Block.

Rows 46-58: Repeat Rows 44 and 45, 6 times; then repeat Row 44 once **more**: 43 Blocks.

Rows 59-97: Turn; slip st in first 3 dc and in next ch-3 sp, ch 3, 3 dc in same sp, work Blocks across to last Block, slip st in ch-3 sp on last Block: 4 Blocks.

Row 98: Turn; slip st in first 3 dc and in next ch-3 sp, ch 3, 3 dc in same sp, work 2 Blocks, slip st in ch-3 sp on last Block: 3 Blocks.

Row 99: Turn; slip st in first 3 dc and in next ch-3 sp, ch 3, 3 dc in same sp, work Block, slip st in ch-3 sp on last Block: 2 Blocks.

Row 100: Turn; slip st in first 3 dc and in next ch-3 sp, ch 3, 3 dc in same sp, slip st in ch-3 sp on last Block; do **not** finish off: one Block.

EDGING

Rnd 1: Ch 1, turn; sc evenly around entire Body working 3 sc in each corner; join with slip st to first sc.

Rnd 2: Ch 1, do **not** turn; sc in each sc around working 3 sc in center sc of each corner 3-sc group; join with slip st to first sc, finish off.

Rnd 3: With **right** side facing, join Blue with sc in center sc of any corner 3-sc group ***(see Joining With Sc, page 21)***; 2 sc in same st as joining, sc in each sc around working 3 sc in center sc of each corner 3-sc group; join with slip st to first sc.

Rnd 4: Ch 1, working from **left** to **right**, work reverse sc in each sc around ***(Figs. 2a-d, page 22)***; join with slip st to first st, finish off.

CHART

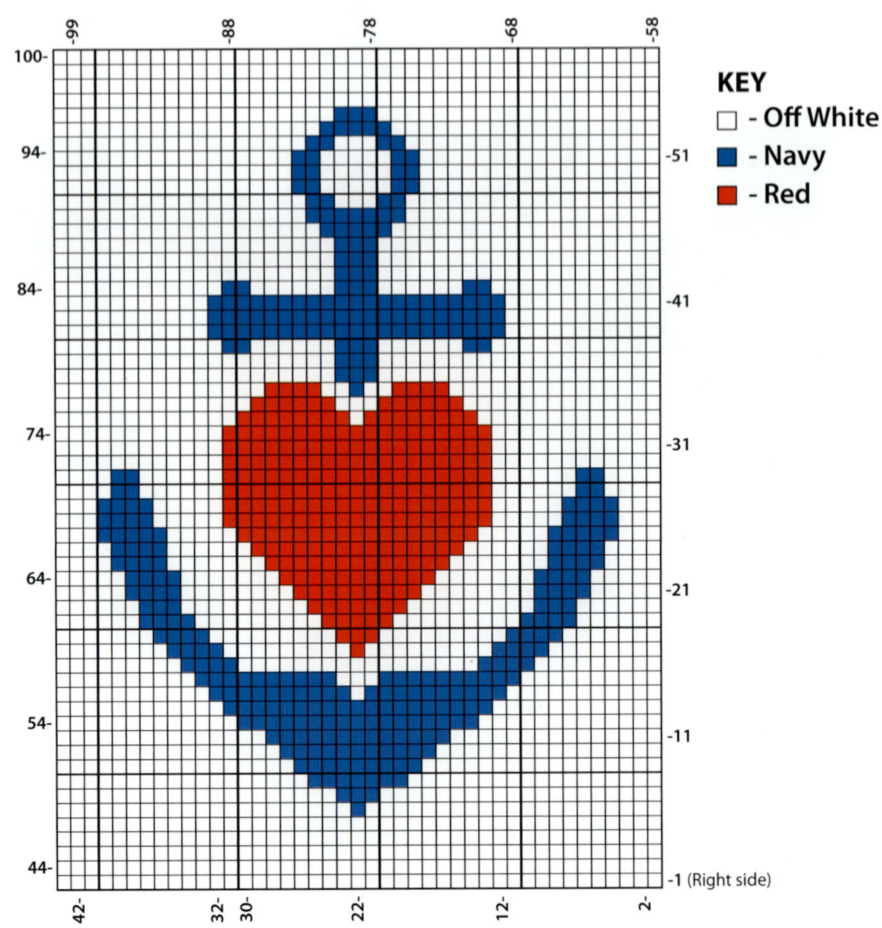

Pebble

EASY

Shown on page 7.

Finished Size: 17½" x 23" (44.5 cm x 58.5 cm)

SHOPPING LIST

Yarn (Light Weight) LIGHT 3

[2.6 ounces, 173 yards
(75 grams, 158 meters) per skein]:

- ☐ Blue - 1 skein
- ☐ Yellow - 1 skein
- ☐ Red - 1 skein
- ☐ Cream - 1 skein

Crochet Hook

- ☐ Size H (5 mm)
  or size needed for gauge

GAUGE INFORMATION

In pattern, 16 sts and 14 rows = 4" (10 cm)
Gauge Swatch: 2" x 2" x 3"
(5 cm x 5 cm x 7.5 cm)
Work same as Body for 6 rows: 12 sts.

STITCH GUIDE

SINGLE CROCHET 2 TOGETHER
(abbreviated sc2tog)
Pull up a loop in each of next 2 sts, YO and draw through all 3 loops on hook **(counts as one sc)**.

BODY

Body is worked diagonally.

Row 1: With Blue, ch 2, 2 sc in second ch from hook.

Row 2 (Right side)**:** Ch 2 **(does not count as a st, now and throughout)**, turn; (dc, sc) in each sc across: 4 sts.

Note: Loop a short piece of yarn around any stitch to mark Row 2 as **right** side.

Row 3: Ch 2, turn; (dc, sc) in first sc, dc in next dc, sc in next sc, (dc, sc) in last dc: 6 sts.

Rows 4-7: Ch 2, turn; (dc, sc) in first sc, (dc in next dc, sc in next sc) across to last dc, (dc, sc) in last dc: 14 sts.

Row 8: Ch 2, turn; (dc, sc) in first sc, (dc in next dc, sc in next sc) across to last dc, (dc, sc) in last dc, changing to Cream in last sc *(Fig. 1a, page 22)*; cut old color: 16 sts.

Rows 9 and 10: Repeat Rows 7 and 8; at end of Row 10, change to Yellow: 20 sts.

Rows 11-17: Repeat Row 4, 7 times: 34 sts.

Row 18: Repeat Row 8: 36 sts.

Rows 19 and 20: Repeat Rows 7 and 8; at end of Row 20, change to Red: 40 sts.

Rows 21-27: Repeat Row 4, 7 times: 54 sts.

Row 28: Repeat Row 8: 56 sts.

Rows 29 and 30: Repeat Rows 7 and 8; at end of Row 30, change to Blue: 60 sts.

Rows 31-37: Repeat Row 4, 7 times: 74 sts.

Row 38: Repeat Row 8: 76 sts.

Rows 39 and 40: Repeat Rows 7 and 8; at end of Row 40, change to Yellow: 80 sts.

Rows 41-47: Repeat Row 4, 7 times: 94 sts.

Row 48: Repeat Row 8: 96 sts.

Row 49: Ch 2, turn; (dc, sc) in first sc, dc in next dc, (sc in next sc, dc in next dc) across to last 2 sts, sc2tog.

Row 50: Ch 2, turn; skip first sc, (dc in next dc, sc in next sc) across to last dc, (dc, sc) in last dc, changing to Red in last sc; cut old color.

Row 51: Ch 2, turn; (dc, sc) in first sc, dc in next dc, (sc in next sc, dc in next dc) across to last 2 sts, sc2tog.

Row 52: Ch 2, turn; skip first sc, (dc in next dc, sc in next sc) across to last dc, (dc, sc) in last dc.

Rows 53-58: Repeat Rows 51 and 52, 3 times; at end of Row 58, change to Cream; cut old color.

Rows 59 and 60: Repeat Rows 49 and 50; at end of Row 60, change to Yellow.

Row 61: Repeat Row 51.

Rows 62-67 (Decrease rows)**:** Ch 2, turn; skip first sc, dc in next dc, (sc in next sc, dc in next dc) across to last 2 sts, sc2tog: 84 sts.

Row 68 (Decrease row)**:** Ch 2, turn; skip first sc, dc in next dc, (sc in next sc, dc in next dc) across to last 2 sts, sc2tog changing to Cream; cut old color: 82 sts.

Rows 69 and 70: Repeat Rows 67 and 68; at end of Row 70, change to Blue: 78 sts.

Rows 71-78: Repeat Row 62, 8 times; at end of Row 78, change to Cream; cut Blue: 62 sts.

Rows 79 and 80: Repeat Rows 67 and 68; at end of Row 80, change to Red: 58 sts.

Rows 81-88: Repeat Row 62, 8 times; at end of Row 88, change to Cream; cut Red: 42 sts.

Rows 89 and 90: Repeat Rows 67 and 68; at end of Row 90, change to Yellow: 38 sts.

Rows 91-98: Repeat Row 62, 8 times; at end of Row 98, change to Cream; cut Yellow: 22 sts.

Rows 99 and 100: Repeat Rows 67 and 68; at end of Row 100, change to Blue: 18 sts.

Rows 101-106: Repeat Row 62, 7 times: 6 sts.

Row 107: Ch 2, turn; skip first sc, dc in next dc, sc in next sc, dc in next dc, sc2tog: 4 sts.

Row 108: Ch 2, turn; skip first sc, dc in next dc, sc2tog; finish off: 2 sts.

Edging Rnd: With **right** side facing, join Cream with sc in any corner ***(see Joining With Sc, page 21)***; (dc, sc) in same st; working in end of rows, (sc, dc, sc) evenly around entire piece; join with slip st to first sc, finish off.

Granny

EASY

Finished Size: 19" x 24½" (48.5 cm x 62 cm)

SHOPPING LIST

Yarn (Light Weight) 3

[5 ounces, 388 yards
(140 grams, 355 meters) per skein]:

☐ 1 skein

Crochet Hook

☐ Size G (4 mm)
or size needed for gauge

GAUGE INFORMATION

(3 dc, ch 1) 4 times = 3¾" (9.5 cm)

Gauge Swatch: 2¾" x 2¾" x 4½"
(7 cm x 7 cm x 11.5 cm)

Work same as Body for 4 rows: 5 ch-1 sps.

BODY

Body is worked diagonally.

Ch 4; join with slip st to form a ring.

Row 1: Ch 4 **(counts as first dc plus ch 1, now and throughout)**, (3 dc, ch 1, dc) in ring: 2 ch-1 sps.

Row 2 (Right side)**:** Ch 4, turn; 3 dc in first ch-1 sp, ch 1, (3 dc, ch 1, dc) in last ch-1 sp, leave last dc unworked **(now and throughout)**: 3 ch-1 sps.

Row 3: Ch 4, turn; 3 dc in first ch-1 sp, ch 1, 3 dc in next ch-1 sp, ch 1, (3 dc, ch 1, dc) in last ch-1 sp: 4 ch-1 sps.

Rows 4-26: Ch 4, turn; 3 dc in first ch-1 sp, ch 1, (3 dc in next ch-1 sp, ch 1) across to last ch-1 sp, (3 dc, ch 1, dc) in last ch-1 sp: 27 ch-1 sps.

Row 27: Ch 4, turn; skip first ch-1 sp, (3 dc in next ch-1 sp, ch 1) across to last ch-1 sp, (3 dc, ch 1, dc) in last ch-1 sp.

Row 28: Ch 4, turn; 3 dc in first ch-1 sp, ch 1, (3 dc in next ch-1 sp, ch 1) across to last ch-1 sp, dc in last ch-1 sp.

Rows 29-34: Repeat Rows 27 and 28, 3 times.

Rows 35-58: Ch 4, turn; skip first ch-1 sp, (3 dc in next ch-1 sp, ch 1) across to last ch-1 sp, dc in last ch-1 sp: 3 ch-1 sps.

Row 59: Ch 4, turn; skip first ch-1 sp, 3 dc in next ch-1 sp, ch 1, dc in last ch-1 sp: 2 ch-1 sps.

Row 60: Ch 2, turn; dc in last ch-1 sp to form last corner; do **not** finish off.

Edging: Ch 1, do **not** turn; (sc, 3 dc) in same sp, ch 1, 3 sc around post of last dc; working in end of rows, † sc in next row, 3 dc in next row, ch 1, 3 sc around post of last dc †; repeat from † to † 15 times **more**, [(sc, 3 dc) in next sp, ch 1, 3 sc around post of last dc made] twice, repeat from † to † 12 times, [(sc, 3 dc) in next sp, ch 1, 3 sc around post of last dc] 3 times, repeat from † to † 16 times, (sc, 3 dc) in next sp, ch 1, 3 sc around post of last dc, repeat from † to † 12 times, (sc, 3 dc) in same sp as first sc; join with slip st to first sc, finish off.

Stripes

■■□□ EASY

Finished Size: 17½" x 22½" (44.5 cm x 57 cm)

SHOPPING LIST

Yarn (Bulky Weight) 5 BULKY

[5 ounces, 110 yards (140 grams, 101 meters) per skein]:

- □ Variegated - 1 skein

[5 ounces, 155 yards (140 grams, 142 meters) per skein]:

- □ Green - 1 skein

Crochet Hook

- □ Size K (6.5 mm)
  or size needed for gauge

GAUGE INFORMATION

8 hdc and 7 rows = 4" (10 cm)

Gauge Swatch: 3½" x 3½" x 4" (9 cm x 9 cm x 10 cm)

Work same as Body for 4 rows: 8 hdc.

BODY

Body is worked diagonally.

Row 1: With Variegated, ch 3, 2 hdc in third ch from hook: 2 hdc.

When changing colors, do **not** cut old yarn; carry loosely along edge.

Row 2 (Right side)**:** Ch 2 **(does not count as a st, now and throughout)**, turn; 2 hdc in each hdc across changing to Green in last hdc *(Fig. 1b, page 22)*, drop Variegated: 4 hdc.

Row 3 (Increase row)**:** Ch 2, turn; 2 hdc in first hdc, hdc in next hdc and in each hdc across to last hdc, 2 hdc in last hdc: 6 hdc.

Row 4 (Increase row)**:** Ch 2, turn; 2 hdc in first hdc, hdc in next hdc and in each hdc across to last hdc, 2 hdc in last hdc changing to Variegated in last hdc, drop Green: 8 hdc.

Row 5 (Increase row)**:** Ch 2, turn; 2 hdc in first hdc, hdc in next hdc and in each hdc across to last hdc, 2 hdc in last hdc: 10 hdc.

Row 6 (Increase row)**:** Ch 2, turn; 2 hdc in first hdc, hdc in next hdc and in each hdc across to last hdc, 2 hdc in last hdc changing to Green in last hdc, drop Variegated: 12 hdc.

Rows 7-22: Repeat Rows 3-6, 4 times: 44 hdc.

Row 23: Ch 2, turn; 2 hdc in first hdc, hdc in next hdc and in each hdc across to last 2 hdc, skip next hdc, hdc in last hdc.

Row 24: Ch 2, turn; skip first hdc, hdc in next hdc and in each hdc across to last hdc, 2 hdc in last hdc changing to Variegated in last hdc, drop Green.

Row 25: Ch 2, turn; 2 hdc in first hdc, hdc in next hdc and in each hdc across to last 2 hdc, skip next hdc, hdc in last hdc.

Row 26: Ch 2, turn; skip first hdc, hdc in next hdc and in each hdc across to last hdc, 2 hdc in last hdc changing to Green in last hdc, drop Variegated.

Rows 27-29: Repeat Rows 23-25.

Row 30 (Decrease row)**:** Ch 2, turn; skip first hdc, hdc in next hdc and in each hdc across to last 2 hdc, skip next hdc, hdc in last hdc changing to Green, drop Variegated: 42 hdc.

Row 31 (Decrease row)**:** Ch 2, turn; skip first hdc, hdc in next hdc and in each hdc across to last 2 hdc, skip next hdc, hdc in last hdc: 40 hdc.

Row 32 (Decrease row)**:** Ch 2, turn; hdc in first hdc, skip next hdc, hdc in next hdc and in each hdc across to last 2 hdc, skip next hdc, hdc in last hdc changing to Variegated, drop Green: 38 hdc.

Row 33 (Decrease row)**:** Ch 2, turn; hdc in first hdc, skip next hdc, hdc in next hdc and in each hdc across to last 2 hdc, skip next hdc, hdc in last hdc: 36 hdc.

Rows 34-49: Repeat Rows 30-33, 4 times: 4 hdc.

Row 50: Ch 2, turn; skip first hdc, hdc in next hdc, skip next hdc, hdc in last hdc changing to Green; cut Variegated: 2 hdc.

EDGING

Rnd 1: Ch 1, do **not** turn; sc evenly around entire Body working 3 sc in each corner; join with slip st to first sc.

Rnd 2: Ch 1, sc in each sc around working 3 sc in center sc of each corner 3-sc group; join with slip st to first sc, finish off.

Single

EASY

Finished Size: 17" x 21" (43 cm x 53.5 cm)

SHOPPING LIST

Yarn (Light Weight) 3

[4.2 ounces, 310 yards
(120 grams, 283 meters) per skein]:

☐ 2 skeins

Crochet Hook

☐ Size K (6.5 mm)
or size needed for gauge

GAUGE INFORMATION

In pattern, 14 sts and 14 rows = 3¼" (8.25 cm)

Gauge Swatch: 3¼" x 3¼" x 4½"
(8.25 cm x 8.25 cm x 11.5 cm)

Work same as Body for 9 rows: 11 sc and 8 ch-1 sps.

STITCH GUIDE

SINGLE CROCHET 2 TOGETHER
(abbreviated sc2tog)
(uses last ch-1 sp and last sc)

Insert hook in last ch-1 sp, YO and pull up a loop, insert hook in last sc, YO and pull up a loop, YO and draw through all 3 loops on hook **(counts as one sc)**.

BODY

Body is worked diagonally.

Row 1 (Right side)**:** Ch 2, 3 sc in second ch from hook.

Row 2: Ch 1, turn; 2 sc in first sc, sc in next sc, 2 sc in last sc: 5 sc.

Row 3: Ch 1, turn; 2 sc in first sc, ch 1, skip next sc, sc in next sc, ch 1, skip next sc, 2 sc in last sc: 5 sc and 2 ch-1 sps.

Row 4: Ch 1, turn; 2 sc in first sc, ch 1, ★ skip next sc, sc in next ch-1 sp, ch 1; repeat from ★ once **more**, skip next sc, 2 sc in last sc: 6 sc and 3 ch-1 sps.

Rows 5-56: Ch 1, turn; 2 sc in first sc, ch 1, ★ skip next sc, sc in next ch-1 sp, ch 1; repeat from ★ across to last 2 sc, skip next sc, 2 sc in last sc: 58 sc and 55 ch-1 sps.

Row 57: Ch 1, turn; 2 sc in first sc, ch 1, ★ skip next sc, sc in next ch-1 sp, ch 1; repeat from ★ across to last 2 sc, skip next sc, sc in last sc: 58 sc and 56 ch-1 sps.

Row 58: Ch 1, turn; skip first sc, sc in next ch-1 sp, ch 1, ★ skip next sc, sc in next ch-1 sp, ch 1; repeat from ★ across to last 2 sc, skip next sc, 2 sc in last sc.

Row 59: Ch 1, turn; 2 sc in first sc, ch 1, ★ skip next sc, sc in next ch-1 sp, ch 1; repeat from ★ across to last ch-1 sp, sc2tog.

Rows 60-69: Repeat Rows 58 and 59, 5 times.

Row 70: Ch 1, turn; skip first sc, sc in next ch-1-sp, ch 1, ★ skip next sc, sc in next ch-1 sp, ch 1; repeat from ★ across to last ch-1 sp, insert hook in last ch-1 sp, YO and pull up a loop, skip next sc, insert hook in last sc, YO and pull up a loop, YO and draw through all 3 loops on hook **(counts as one sc)**: 57 sc and 56 ch-1 sps.

Rows 71-123: Ch 1, turn; skip first sc, sc in next ch-1-sp, ch 1, ★ skip next sc, sc in next ch-1 sp, ch 1; repeat from ★ across to last ch-1 sp, sc2tog: 4 sc and 3 ch-1 sps.

Row 124: Ch 1, turn; skip first sc, sc in next ch-1-sp, ch 1, skip next sc, sc in next ch-1 sp, ch 1, skip next sc, sc2tog: 3 sc and 2 ch-1 sps.

Row 125: Ch 1, turn; skip first sc, sc in next ch-1-sp, ch 1, skip next sc, sc2tog: 2 sc.

Edging Rnd: Ch 1, do **not** turn; (sc, ch 2, sc) in st or row evenly around entire Body; join with slip st to first sc, finish off.

Traditional

EASY

Finished Size: 17½" x 22½" (44.5 cm x 57 cm)

SHOPPING LIST

Yarn (Light Weight) LIGHT 3

[4.5 ounces, 318 yards

(127 grams, 290 meters) per skein]:

- ☐ Grey - 1 skein
- ☐ Lilac - 1 skein
- ☐ Peach - 1 skein
- ☐ Green - 1 skein
- ☐ Blue - 1 skein

Crochet Hook

- ☐ Size H (5 mm)

  or size needed for gauge

GAUGE INFORMATION

4 Blocks (side by side) = 3" (7.5 cm)

Gauge Swatch: 3" x 3" x 4"

(7.5 cm x 7.5 cm x 10 cm)

Work same as Body for 4 rows: 4 Blocks.

STITCH GUIDE

BEGINNING BLOCK

Ch 6, turn; dc in fourth ch from hook and in next 2 chs.

BLOCK

Slip st in ch-3 sp of previous Block ***(Fig. A, page 2)***, ch 3, 3 dc in same sp ***(Fig. B, page 2)***.

BODY

Body is worked diagonally.

Row 1 (Right side)**:** With Grey, ch 6, dc in fourth ch from hook and in last 2 chs: one Block.

Row 2: Work Beginning Block, slip st in ch-3 sp on first Block, ch 3, 3 dc in same sp: 2 Blocks.

Row 3: Work Beginning Block, slip st in ch-3 sp on first Block, ch 3, 3 dc in same sp, work Block: 3 Blocks.

Row 4: Work Beginning Block, slip st in ch-3 sp on first Block, ch 3, 3 dc in same sp, work Blocks across changing to Blue in last dc ***(Fig. 1c, page 22)***; cut Grey: 4 Blocks.

Rows 5-9: Work Beginning Block, slip st in ch-3 sp on first Block, ch 3, 3 dc in same sp, work Blocks across: 9 Blocks.

Row 10: Work Beginning Block, slip st in ch-3 sp on first Block, ch 3, 3 dc in same sp, work Blocks across changing to Grey in last dc; cut Blue: 10 Blocks.

Row 11: Work Beginning Block, slip st in ch-3 sp on first Block, ch 3, 3 dc in same sp, work Blocks across: 11 Blocks.

Row 12: Work Beginning Block, slip st in ch-3 sp on first Block, ch 3, 3 dc in same sp, work Blocks across changing to Peach in last dc; cut Grey: 12 Blocks.

Rows 13-17: Work Beginning Block, slip st in ch-3 sp on first Block, ch 3, 3 dc in same sp, work Blocks across: 17 Blocks.

Row 18: Work Beginning Block, slip st in ch-3 sp on first Block, ch 3, 3 dc in same sp, work Blocks across changing to Grey in last dc; cut Peach: 18 Blocks.

Row 19: Work Beginning Block, slip st in ch-3 sp on first Block, ch 3, 3 dc in same sp, work Blocks across: 19 Blocks.

Row 20: Work Beginning Block, slip st in ch-3 sp on first Block, ch 3, 3 dc in same sp, work Blocks across changing to Purple in last dc; cut Grey: 20 Blocks.

Rows 21-25: Work Beginning Block, slip st in ch-3 sp on first Block, ch 3, 3 dc in same sp, work Blocks across: 25 Blocks.

Row 26: Work Beginning Block, slip st in ch-3 sp on first Block, ch 3, 3 dc in same sp, work Blocks across changing to Grey in last dc; cut Purple: 26 Blocks.

Row 27: Work Beginning Block, slip st in ch-3 sp on first Block, ch 3, 3 dc in same sp, work Blocks across: 27 Blocks.

Row 28: Turn; slip st in first 3 dc and in next ch-3 sp, ch 3, 3 dc in same sp, work Blocks across changing to Green in last dc; cut Grey.

Row 29: Work Beginning Block, slip st in ch-3 sp on first Block, ch 3, 3 dc in same sp, work Blocks across to last Block, slip st in ch-3 sp on last Block.

Row 30: Turn; slip st in first 3 dc and in next ch-3 sp, ch 3, 3 dc in same sp, work Blocks across.

Rows 31-33: Repeat Rows 29 and 30 once, then repeat Row 29 once **more**.

Row 34: Turn; slip st in first 3 dc and in next ch-3 sp, ch 3, 3 dc in same sp, work Blocks across changing to Grey in last dc; cut Green.

Rows 35 and 36: Repeat Rows 29 and 30.

Row 37: Turn; slip st in first 3 dc and in next ch-3 sp changing to Purple in last slip st made; cut Grey, ch 3, 3 dc in same sp, work Blocks across to last Block, slip st in ch-3 sp on last Block: 26 Blocks.

Rows 38-42: Turn; slip st in first 3 dc and in next ch-3 sp, ch 3, 3 dc in same sp, work Blocks across to last Block, slip st in ch-3 sp on last Block: 21 Blocks.

Row 43 (Decrease row)**:** Turn; slip st in first 3 dc and in next ch-3 sp changing to Grey in last slip st made; cut old color, ch 3, 3 dc in same sp, work Blocks across to last Block, slip st in ch-3 sp on last Block: 20 Blocks.

Row 44 (Decrease row)**:** Turn; slip st in first 3 dc and in next ch-3 sp, ch 3, 3 dc in same sp, work Blocks across to last Block, slip st in ch-3 sp on last Block: 19 Blocks.

Row 45: Turn; slip st in first 3 dc and in next ch-3 sp changing to Peach in last slip st made; cut Grey, ch 3, 3 dc in same sp, work Blocks across to last Block, slip st in ch-3 sp on last Block: 18 Blocks.

Rows 46-50: Repeat Row 44, 5 times: 13 Blocks.

Rows 51 and 52: Repeat Rows 43 and 44: 11 Blocks.

Row 53: Turn; slip st in first 3 dc and in next ch-3 sp changing to Blue in last slip st made; cut Grey, ch 3, 3 dc in same sp, work Blocks across to last Block, slip st in ch-3 sp on last Block: 10 Blocks.

Rows 54-58: Repeat Row 44, 5 times: 5 Blocks.

Row 59: Repeat Row 43: 4 Blocks.

Row 60: Turn; slip st in first 3 dc and in next ch-3 sp, ch 3, 3 dc in same sp, work 2 Blocks, slip st in ch-3 sp on last Block: 3 Blocks.

Row 61: Turn; slip st in first 3 dc and in next ch-3 sp, ch 3, 3 dc in same sp, work Block, slip st in ch-3 sp on last Block: 2 Blocks.

Row 62: Turn; slip st in first 3 dc and in next ch-3 sp, ch 3, 3 dc in same sp, slip st in ch-3 sp on last Block; do **not** finish off: one Block.

EDGING

Rnd 1: Ch 1, turn; sc evenly around entire Body, working 3 sc in each corner; join with slip st to first sc.

Rnd 2: Ch 1, working from **left** to **right**, work reverse sc in each sc around ***(Figs. 2a-d, page 22)***; join with slip st to first sc, finish off.

Ice Cream

EASY

Finished Size: 37½" x 44½"
(95.5 cm x 113 cm)

SHOPPING LIST

Yarn (Light Weight) LIGHT 3

[5 ounces, 362 yards
(140 grams, 331 meters)
per skein]:

- ☐ White - 5 skeins
- ☐ Pink - 1 skein

[4.2 ounces, 310 yards
(120 grams, 283 meters)
per skein]:

- ☐ Variegated - 1 skein

[1.75 ounces, 161 yards
(50 grams, 147 meters) per skein]:

- ☐ Tan - 1 skein

Crochet Hook

- ☐ Size G (4 mm)
  or size needed for gauge

Additional Supplies

- ☐ Bobbins

GAUGE INFORMATION

5 Blocks (side by side) = 3¼"
(8.25 cm)

Gauge Swatch: 3¼" x 3¼" x 4½"
(8.25 cm x 8.25 cm x 11.5 cm)

Work same as Body for 5 rows:
5 Blocks.

STITCH GUIDE

BEGINNING BLOCK

Ch 6, turn; dc in fourth ch from hook and in next 2 chs.

BLOCK

Slip st in ch-3 sp of previous Block *(Fig. A, page 2)*, ch 3, 3 dc in same sp *(Fig. B, page 2)*.

BODY

Body is worked diagonally.

Row 1 (Right side)**:** With White, ch 6, dc in fourth ch from hook and in last 2 chs: one Block.

Note: Loop a short piece of yarn around any stitch to mark Row 1 as **right** side **and** bottom corner.

Row 2: Work Beginning Block, slip st in ch-3 sp on first Block, ch 3, 3 dc in same sp: 2 Blocks.

Row 3: Work Beginning Block, slip st in ch-3 sp on first Block, ch 3, 3 dc in same sp, work Block: 3 Blocks.

Rows 4-32: Work Beginning Block, slip st in ch-3 sp on first Block, ch 3, 3 dc in same sp, work Blocks across: 32 Blocks.

Row 33: Work Beginning Block, slip st in ch-3 sp on first Block, ch 3, 3 dc in same sp, work 27 Blocks, changing to Tan in last dc made *(Fig. 1c, page 22)*, work Block changing to White in last dc made, work Blocks across: 33 Blocks.

Always change colors in same manner, using bobbins for small sections of color. Keep unused color to **wrong** side of work; do **not** cut yarn until color is no longer needed.

Continue to follow Chart on page 20 throughout.

Rows 34-60: Work Beginning Block, slip st in ch-3 sp on first Block, ch 3, 3 dc in same sp, work Blocks across: 60 Blocks.

Row 61: Work Beginning Block, slip st in ch-3 sp on first Block, ch 3, 3 dc in same sp, work Blocks across to last Block, slip st in ch-3 sp on last Block.

Row 62: Turn; slip st in first 3 dc and in next ch-3 sp, ch 3, 3 dc in same sp, work Blocks across.

Rows 63-72: Repeat Rows 61 and 62, 5 times.

Rows 73-128: Turn; slip st in first 3 dc and in next ch-3 sp, ch 3, 3 dc in same sp, work Blocks across to last Block, slip st in ch-3 sp on last Block: 4 Blocks.

Row 129: Turn; slip st in first 3 dc and in next ch-3 sp, ch 3, 3 dc in same sp, work 2 Blocks, slip st in ch-3 sp on last Block: 3 Blocks.

Row 130: Turn; slip st in first 3 dc and in next ch-3 sp, ch 3, 3 dc in same sp, work Block, slip st in ch-3 sp on last Block: 2 Blocks.

Row 131: Turn; slip st in first 3 dc and in next ch-3 sp, ch 3, 3 dc in same sp, slip st in ch-3 sp on last Block; do **not** finish off: one Block.

EDGING

Rnd 1: Ch 1, do **not** turn; sc evenly around entire Body working 3 sc in each corner; join with slip st to first sc.

Rnd 2: Ch 1, sc in each sc around working 3 sc in center sc of each corner 3-sc group; join with slip st to first sc, finish off.

Rnd 3: With **right** side facing, join Pink with sc in center sc of any corner 3-sc group ***(see Joining With Sc, page 21)***; 2 sc in same st as joining, sc in each sc around working 3 sc in center sc of each corner 3-sc group; join with slip st to first sc.

Rnd 4: Ch 1, working from **left** to **right**, work reverse sc in each sc around ***(Figs. 2a-d, page 22)***; join with slip st to first st, finish off.

KEY

☐ - White
☐ - Pink
☐ - Variegated
☐ - Tan

CHART

General Instructions

ABBREVIATIONS

ch(s)	chain(s)
cm	centimeters
dc	double crochet(s)
hdc	half double crochet(s)
mm	millimeters
Rnd(s)	Round(s)
sc	single crochet(s)
sc2tog	single crochet 2 together
sp(s)	space(s)
st(s)	stitch(es)
YO	yarn over

CROCHET TERMINOLOGY		
UNITED STATES		INTERNATIONAL
slip stitch (slip st)	=	single crochet (sc)
single crochet (sc)	=	double crochet (dc)
half double crochet (hdc)	=	half treble crochet (htr)
double crochet (dc)	=	treble crochet (tr)
treble crochet (tr)	=	double treble crochet (dtr)
double treble crochet (dtr)	=	triple treble crochet (ttr)
triple treble crochet (tr tr)	=	quadruple treble crochet (qtr)
skip	=	miss

SYMBOLS & TERMS

★ — work instructions following ★ as many **more** times as indicated in addition to the first time.

† to † — work all instructions from first † to second † **as many** times as specified.

( ) or **[ ]** — work enclosed instructions **as many** times as specified by the number immediately following **or** work all enclosed instructions in the stitch or space indicated **or** contains explanatory remarks.

colon (:) — the number(s) given after a colon at the end of a row or round denote(s) the number of stitches or spaces you should have on that row or round.

GAUGE

Exact gauge is **essential** for proper size. Before beginning your project, make the sample swatch given in the individual instructions in the yarn and hook specified. After completing the swatch, measure it, counting your stitches and rows carefully. If your swatch is larger or smaller than specified, **make another, changing hook size to get the correct gauge**. Keep trying until you find the size hook that will give you the specified gauge.

JOINING WITH SC

When instructed to join with sc, begin with a slip knot on hook. Insert hook in stitch or space indicated, YO and pull up a loop, YO and draw through both loops on hook.

CROCHET HOOKS																	
U.S.	B-1	C-2	D-3	E-4	F-5	G-6	7	H-8	I-9	J-10	K-10½	L-11	M/N-13	N/P-15	P/Q	Q	S
Metric - mm	2.25	2.75	3.25	3.5	3.75	4	4.5	5	5.5	6	6.5	8	9	10	15	16	19

BEGINNER	Projects for first-time crocheters using basic stitches. Minimal shaping.
EASY	Projects using yarn with basic stitches, repetitive stitch patterns, simple color changes, and simple shaping and finishing.
INTERMEDIATE	Projects using a variety of techniques, such as basic lace patterns or color patterns, mid-level shaping and finishing.
EXPERIENCED	Projects with intricate stitch patterns, techniques and dimension, such as non-repeating patterns, multi-color techniques, fine threads, small hooks, detailed shaping and refined finishing.

CHANGING COLORS

Work the last stitch to within one step of completion, hook new yarn *(Fig. 1a, 1b or 1c)* and draw though all loops on hook.

Fig. 1a

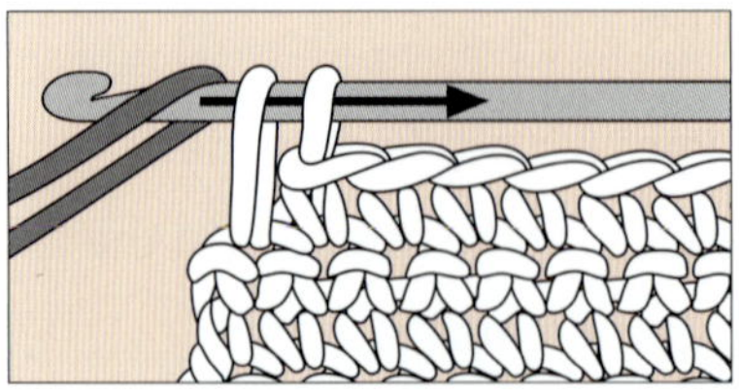

Fig. 1b

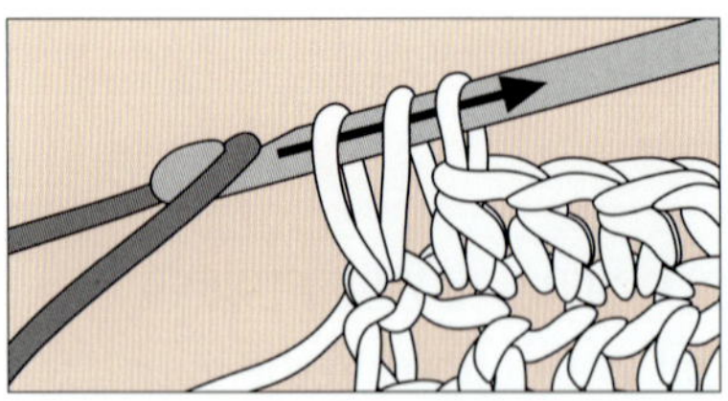

Fig. 1c

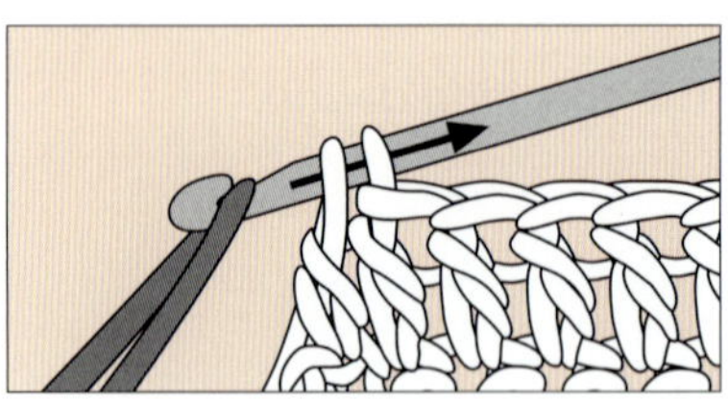

REVERSE SINGLE CROCHET

(abbreviated reverse sc)

Working from **left** to **right**, ★ insert hook in st to right of hook ***(Fig. 2a)***, YO and draw through, under and to left of loop on hook (2 loops on hook) ***(Fig. 2b)***, YO and draw through both loops on hook ***(Fig. 2c)*** **(reverse sc made, *Fig. 2d*)**; repeat from ★ around.

Fig. 2a

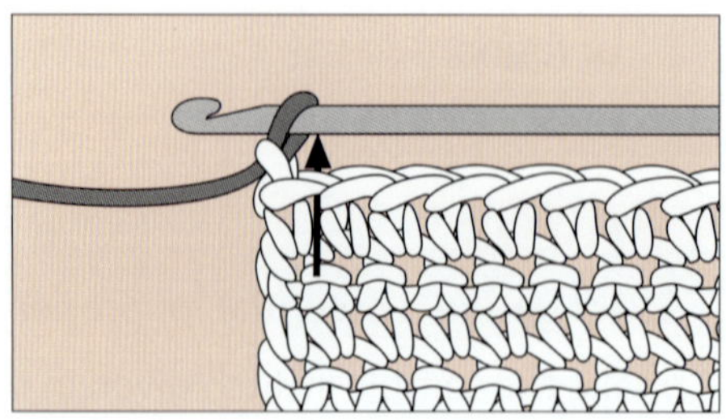

Fig. 2b

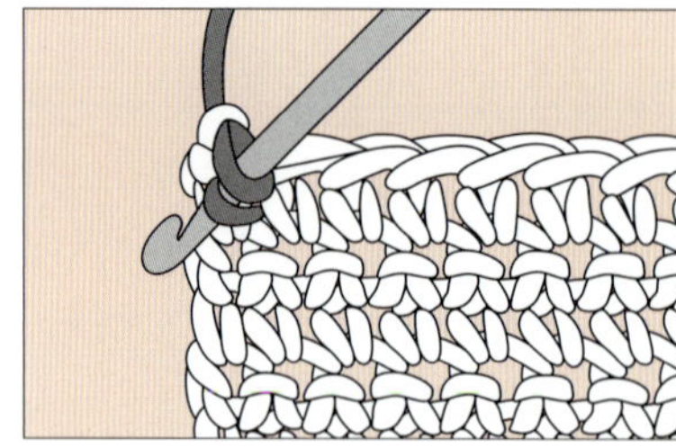

Fig. 2c

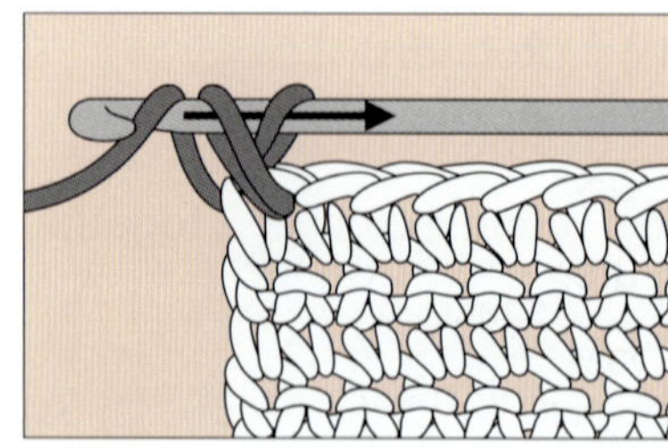

Fig. 2d

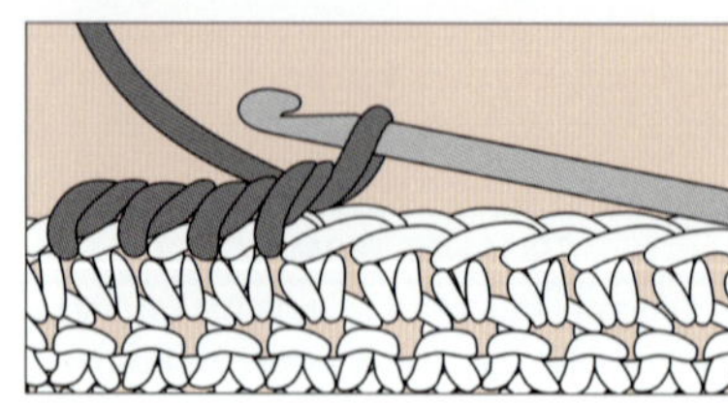

Yarn Weight Symbol & Names	LACE 0	SUPER FINE 1	FINE 2	LIGHT 3	MEDIUM 4	BULKY 5	SUPER BULKY 6	JUMBO 7
Type of Yarns in Category	Fingering, size 10 crochet thread	Sock, Fingering, Baby	Sport, Baby	DK, Light Worsted	Worsted, Afghan, Aran	Chunky, Craft, Rug	Super Bulky, Roving	Jumbo, Roving
Crochet Gauge* Ranges in Single Crochet to 4" (10 cm)	32-42 sts**	21-32 sts	16-20 sts	12-17 sts	11-14 sts	8-11 sts	6-9 sts	5 sts and fewer
Advised Hook Size Range	Steel*** 6 to 8, Regular hook B-1	B-1 to E-4	E-4 to 7	7 to I-9	I-9 to K-10½	K-10½ to M/N-13	M/N-13 to Q	Q and larger

*GUIDELINES ONLY: The chart above reflects the most commonly used gauges and hook sizes for specific yarn categories.

** Lace weight yarns are usually crocheted with larger hooks to create lacy openwork patterns. Accordingly, a gauge range is difficult to determine. Always follow the gauge stated in your pattern.

*** Steel crochet hooks are sized differently from regular hooks–the higher the number, the smaller the hook, which is the reverse of regular hook sizing.

Yarn Information

The Afghans in this book were made using a variety of yarn weights. Any brand of the specified yarn weight may be used. It is best to refer to the yardage/meters when determining how many balls or skeins to purchase. Remember, to arrive at the finished size, it is the GAUGE/TENSION that is important, not the brand of yarn.

For your convenience, listed below are the specific yarns used to create our photography models. Because yarn manufacturers make frequent changes in their product lines, you may sometimes find it necessary to use a substitute yarn or to search for the discontinued product at alternate suppliers (locally or online).

ANCHOR
Red Heart® Soft®
Off White - #4601 Off White
Red - #5142 Cherry Red
Red Heart® Soft Baby Steps®
Navy - #9851 Navy

PEBBLE
Lion Brand® Modern Baby®
Blue - #109 Blue
Yellow - #158 Yellow
Red - #113 Red
Cream - #098 Cream

GRANNY
Bernat® Baby Coordinates™
#48046 Soft Grey

STRIPES
Baby Bee® Angel Fleece™
Variegated - #1151 Crayons
Bernat® Softee® Baby Chunky™
Green - #96004 Surf Green

SINGLE
Bernat® Softee® Baby™
#31425 Princess Pebbles Ombre

TRADITIONAL
Red Heart® Baby Hugs™ Light
Grey - #3410 Dolphin
Lilac - #3538 Lilac
Peach - #3258 Peachie
Green - #3562 Aloe
Blue - #3825 Bluie

ICE CREAM
Bernat® Softee® Baby™
White - #02000 White
Pink - #30205 Prettiest Pink
Variegated -
#31415 Candy Baby Ombre
Patons® Astra™
Tan - #02020 Medium Tan

We have made every effort to ensure that these instructions are accurate and complete.
We cannot, however, be responsible for human error, typographical mistakes, or variations in individual work.

Production Team: Instructional/Technical Writer - Lois J. Long; Editorial Writer - Susan Frantz Wiles; Senior Graphic Artist - Lora Puls; Graphic Artist - Kellie McAnulty; Photo Stylist - Lori Wenger; and Photographer - Jason Masters.

Meet Becky Stevens

Becky Stevens made the move from her home state of Pennsylvania to Maryland more than 40 years ago — which was about the time she started crocheting. She's learned so much about the skill since then that she teaches a weekly group in her home and holds an annual workshop at a New York lake resort. Becky says, "I think the most rewarding things about crochet are relaxing with your project and seeing the final result, especially when making a very personal, thoughtful gift."

Other Leisure Arts books featuring Becky's designs include *Sweet Stripes for Baby* (#6756), *Baby's Diagonal Aran Afghans* (#5732), *Crochet Car Seat Blankets* (#75469), *Knit Car Seat Blankets* (#75470), *Hats and Scarves for the Family* (#75499), *Cozy Fashion Accents* (#6658), *Tunisian Dishcloths* (#6371), and *Panel by Panel Afghans* (#4814).